THE PASTORAL MINISTRY
OF CHURCH OFFICERS

THE
PASTORAL
MINISTRY
OF
CHURCH OFFICERS

by *Charlie W. Shedd*

JOHN KNOX PRESS
Richmond, Virginia

Fifth printing 1971

International Standard Book Number: 0–8042–1788–2

Library of Congress Catalog Card Number: 65–11504

© M. E. Bratcher 1965

Printed in the United States of America

Contents

I

CALLED
TO MINISTER

This story is true. It is about Emma, a housewife, and George, an officer in her church. Only their names have been changed to protect the real people. There are dozens of these little background dramas in the life of any church. This one is recorded here as a tip of the hat to thousands of faithful servants in the advance guard of man's long march to the City of God.

There are some people whose very presence seems to pull things together. Emma was one of these. She was president of the Women of the Church the year they reorganized. As though that were not enough, it was also the year for moving into the new building, and she had to settle the unfortunate fuss over the colors in the kitchen.

It was a very hard year. For one thing, there were some of the old-timers who did not like the idea of building in the first place, and they most certainly wanted no part of reorganization. As one poet says, "They had ruled the roost a hundred years or so and to every new proposal they had always answered, 'No.' "

Then there was the new group, some bewildered by the pounds of paper and ink, some frankly quite uninterested, some jockeying for position. There was also the customary tyranny of details —phone calls and visits, announcements and reports, committees and meetings. But through it all Emma moved like a queen. She compromised in matters unimportant, stood her ground in things that counted, deftly handled the opposition, and where she felt herself inadequate asked the Lord to make her tall enough for her crown. And he did.

Then there was George. He was an Elder, who, eleven years before, took seriously his charge to "watch diligently over the flock." Being so sensitive to God's calling, he moved right in when he heard about the tragedy. He remembered well the day this young couple had come before the Session for membership. Now they were taking the young wife away, and they didn't know whether she'd ever be back with her family. Six weeks after the baby was born, Emma had gone completely out of her mind, and the doctor said the only safe place was the state hospital for the mentally ill. In her present state of mind she might destroy her child. She might even turn against her husband, or her parents, or one of the neighbors. So they took her away.

Word came back occasionally that there was no change, and it looked like a permanent loss. Her parents took the child. The young husband came alone to church, and the embers of concern seemed to die with the weeks as these things do.

But they did not die in George's heart. In addition to a natural warm tendency, he had been elected by the congregation to "visit the people at their homes, especially the sick." So he went now and then to see the young father, checked up occasionally on the baby, and paid a visit to the doctor. Since he made occasional sales trips in that direction, he wanted to know if it would be all right for him to stop at the hospital and express the concern of the church.

To dash quickly now across the weeks and months, he received permission through proper channels, and he stopped. The first time, it was not one of her good days, so he left his card with a scribbled note, "We're praying for you at the church."

On succeeding visits they brought her in to visit for a few moments across the fenced table. At first she showed little interest. But George refused to give up. He would talk a bit about the lilacs in bloom at her house; about the new front on his hardware store; or describe how the high school team had won the district championship.

Then one day she asked about the baby and her husband. For just a moment George thought he saw a flicker of her former self.

For several more months he continued to drop in when he was

over that way. Each time she showed more interest, and each time he left, George would add simply, "We're praying for you at the church."

Then one day he received a letter which said he wouldn't need to stop any more. *She was coming home for Christmas.* The doctor said that if everything went well he'd let her stay. How could she ever tell him what his visits had meant, and would he please express her thanks to the church for their prayers? She hoped she'd be worthy of their love.

So Emma came home. That year, there was something new about Christmas in the town. And it seemed that no people of God ever sang quite like our congregation as they joined in the old carol: "And ye, beneath life's crushing load, / Whose forms are bending low, / Who toil along the climbing way / With painful steps and slow, / Look now! for glad and golden hours / Come swiftly on the wing: / O rest beside the weary road, / And hear the angels sing."

This is a true story. It actually took place in a congregation where the author watched the miracle unfold. What really happened? Was the church responsible or would it have come about anyway as a natural event in the passing of time? Could the actual cure have been attributable to some wise doctor's therapy? Might it have been the work of a new wonder drug?

To all these questions comes the same monotonous answer: We do not know some things for sure! But this is for certain— some healings do wait for human agents to serve as channels for the miracle. One faithful Elder "discharged by the law of love" his high calling. Eleven years later Emma became president of the Women of the Church at a hard time. *Some of us prefer to believe that the church is truly an instrument of God's redeeming love when men and women take seriously their call to serve the Lord in the Household of Faith.*

Here is a quotation from a Board executive in Richmond, Virginia. He spends considerable time visiting churches and he gives a great deal of thought to analyzing the needs of the whole

Household of God. He sees things both in denominational scope and in local focus. He puts a finger on one of our sorest spots when he says:

> I have felt for many months that the elders and deacons of our church did not understand that they have a major mission to perform with reference to this area of the church's life. Possibly it is due to the fact that ministers do not get this point across in training officers, or it may be that they just lapse back into the attitude to let the preacher or another professional do the work. I know this seems to be the case in my own church where I am an elder. Those of us on the Session and the Board of Deacons have a tendency to think that the church's paid staff has more time than any of us for this type of thing. It has been my feeling for many months in my own particular church, as well as for churches throughout the Assembly, that it is not going to show any major life until the elders and deacons do what they are supposed to do. . . . Each minister, as he goes about his pastoral work, realizes how much needs to be done and how limited his own time and energy is to do it all. Somehow we must impress on our elders and deacons that a major responsibility for them is in helping their pastor perform this vital service to individuals in and out of a particular congregation.

The remainder of this book will be given to considering the challenge of that Board executive. Most of us as church officers know that the man has zeroed in on a big void. We may have done a fine job in carrying out the ordinary responsibilities of our office. We may have governed well, voted well, taught well, guided well, financed well, planned well. We may have represented our church well in higher courts and upped our congregational benevolences one hundred percent. We may have honored the office in every customary way. But his question simply will not go away and leave us alone.

How well have we pushed down the partition between the Session room and the homes of our parish? Do we knock on enough doors? Do we cross enough thresholds? Do our members know that their leaders care not only about the church but about the inner personal needs in individual souls?

The *Book of Church Order* leaves no question here. In its direction to Elders it says:

It belongs to their office, both individually and jointly, to watch diligently over the congregation committed to their charge ... They should visit the people at their homes, especially the sick; they should instruct the ignorant, comfort the mourner, nourish and guard the children of the Church. They should pray with and for the people. They should be careful and diligent in seeking the fruit of the preached Word. They should inform the Pastor of cases of sickness, affliction and awakening, and of all others which may need his special attention. . . . All those duties which private Christians are bound to discharge by the law of love are especially incumbent upon the Ruling Elders by reason of their vocation to office, and are to be discharged as official duties. (§11–4)

In its direction to Deacons it is equally lucid:

It is the duty of the Deacons, first of all, to minister to those who are in need, to the sick, to the friendless, and to any who may be in distress. (§12–3)

We have seen what happened when one Elder in one church took seriously his charge to "nourish and guard the children of the Church." We have heard the call of one Board executive who, from his vantage point as overseer to the church at large, cries out for church officers who know their responsibility in ministry. We have read the record of our official law and order. Before we move on to the next chapter, we might do well to pause for a quiet time of prayer as we listen to words direct from the Lord. Suggested Scripture meditations:

James 1:27   James 5:14–16
1 Peter 4:8–10   1 Peter 5:1–4
Ephesians 4:29   Romans 15:1
John 21:15–17   Isaiah 58:10

II

PRINCIPLES

Webster's dictionary presents several meanings of the word "principle." The preferable one for our consideration in this chapter is "A source or origin . . . ultimate basis or cause." We will deal here with several basic principles behind the pastoral ministry of church officers. In addition to the words which we have cited from the *Book of Church Order,* there are even more serious reasons why lay leaders of the Christian church must give themselves to this calling.

1. The purest "source or origin" for any type of Christian ministry is this: *Jesus was concerned about persons!*

One of the threats which must be faced in almost any church is the danger of folks getting lost in the membership.

Critics of modern America observe that "jumbo-itis" tends to be a real flaw in our thinking. We fall into the trap of assuming that it has to be large in order to be good. The same "numerical neurosis" threatens the church. When we listen in the halls at a meeting of our church courts, or in any gathering of laymen and ministers, one often-heard question is: "How many members do you have now?" This tendency to have larger churches may even increase in the future with the impending shortage of ministers. But this bent in the direction of largeness is all the more reason why church leaders must keep this particular principle continually before them—Christ was, and is, a personal Lord and we who would serve him must turn our efforts toward emulating this particular quality in our leadership.

But leaders with experience in churches of various sizes know that this danger is not necessarily limited to large churches. Smaller congregations also know the tragedy of church memberships which took off with enthusiasm but soon dwindled.

Sometimes this demise can be traced to educational failure. There was not enough rootage in training for membership. Perhaps the member did not understand fully all that was involved in becoming a modern-day disciple. Maybe he was not challenged soon enough to make a vital contribution in the work of the church. Perhaps he had an emotional history which did not lend itself to blending easily with any fellowship.

There could be a dozen other reasons. But one of the hardest to face is this possibility: *Maybe the new member, as he progressed in his life with the church, felt no concern for himself as a person!*

I called one day at the hospital following an accident. Two of our members had been seriously hurt in the automobile crash. Before going to their rooms, I asked the nurse at the desk how they were getting along. Her reply was a typical modern-day analysis, "Number 69 is responding to treatment. But number 66 is in serious condition!"

In so many places our up-to-date living is built on these secondary relationships. Life has a way of making us numbers rather than names. We become things instead of people. It is possible for this same impersonalization of the secular world to carry over into the church. If we allow this to happen, the results may be spiritual death for some who desperately need the personal touch of Christ himself on their lives.

When we study the life of Jesus we observe that he had a genius for seeing through "people" to "persons." Others saw a tax-collector—he saw Matthew. His society saw a woman of soiled reputation—he saw Magdalene. The disciples saw a bothersome collection of little people—he saw the precious souls of little children. The fact dominates the Gospels: Jesus was person-conscious!

The church's major reason for existence today is to be an instrument of Christ's reaching out to his own. If we are serious leaders of the church, we will keep continually before us this example of our "source or origin," Christ Jesus himself.

2. A second "ultimate basis or cause" comes clear as we study

the New Testament: *The church which Christ founded was marked by a genuine ministry of the laity.*

On almost every page the New Testament sounds a clear call to the pastoral ministry of those who called themselves followers of Christ:

> By this shall men know that ye are my disciples, if ye have love one to another . . . support the weak . . . visit the fatherless and widows . . . be kindly affectioned one toward another . . . remember the poor . . . feed the flock . . . bear ye one another's burdens . . . lift up the hands which hang down . . . strengthen the brethren . . . remember them that are in bonds . . . as every man hath received the gift, even so minister the same one to another.

Whether it be Christ directing his disciples, the Acts of the Apostles describing life in the early church, or Paul instructing his congregations, there is no escape from this fact—we have a personal responsibility as contemporary Christians to come out of the pews and get into the homes of our parish.

As Christians our number one "source or origin" is Christ himself. But "source or origin" number two for earnest church-men will be a desire to re-create his church in modern society. If we really accomplished this in the absolute, a church with one hundred and fifty members would have one hundred and fifty ministers.

But most of us have a long way to go toward the absolute New Testament church. An examination of most churches today might reveal that we have slipped, without knowing it, into the ways of the world. In some modern churches there is a decided tendency toward over-organization. We are prone to believe that we can't be doing much worthwhile unless we are busy all the time. As one lady put it, "The church is always urging me to create a Christian home. But it assigns me to so many committees that I have no time for the creation."

What would happen in our particular church if the Session decided to put the knife to those things in the program which prevented the "person-to-person" ministry of the New Testament church? Doubtless some things would have to go. But in their going we might rediscover the true character of the family of God.

Throughout the years of our history, have we made a serious mistake as we transferred so much pastoral care to "the man of the cloth"? What would be the effect if we should change our thinking to consider our ordained pastors as "training ministers" and consider our laymen as "the real ministers"? It might be a decided step forward toward a genuine "society of saints" in a world which so desperately needs the Christian gospel demonstrated before its eyes.

Serious contemplation will lead us to see that the early church fathers were standing on center when they wrote:

> All saints being united to Jesus Christ their head, by his Spirit and by faith, have fellowship with him in his graces, sufferings, death, resurrection, and glory: and, being united to one another in love, they have communion in each other's gifts and graces, and are obliged to the performance of such duties, public and private, as do conduce to their mutual good, both in the inward and outward man. (*Confession of Faith,* Ch. XXVIII, Par. 1)

3. A third "ultimate basis or cause" for this service is *the motivating factor of Christian love.*

There is probably no other calling in church leadership responsibility which exceeds this—that a man be an example of love to those who have elected him to this position. The man who has been chosen Elder or Deacon will almost certainly feel that he is unworthy. This is a natural reaction for any person who walks close in the shadow of his Lord. If he accepts, he does so with the prayer that Christ will make him big enough. One place where he will feel the necessity for growth will be in his love resources. If he is sincere in his prayers, he will probably be led to face up to some things within himself which need correction. As he comes to understand that he is to be a leader in love, he will ask Christ to show him those places where he may be blocking the flow of God's love. He can only lead others to love as they should when he has prepared his own heart to love as he should. This is doing business in deep waters, but church officers in our denomination are called to this kind of leadership.

Those who looked at the first church from the outside were amazed at the genuine concern which existed within the covenant community. Their reaction was, "Behold how these Christians love one another!"

This same atmosphere of tender affection will be a mark of the New Testament church reproduced in modern society. Sensitivity of feeling, awareness of need, a genuine helping hand to the weak, redemptive grace for the fallen, sympathy for the frustrated, ears for the lonely, food for the hungry, sorrow shared, and the Good Shepherd's arm extended through human arms—the discerning officer will ask himself whether this kind of love is a part of the climate in his church. If it is not, could it possibly be that the congregation needs this elected person to lead a return of the whole to this "ultimate basis or cause"?

In everything which remains to be said throughout this book, the reader will bear in mind that he cannot "perform" a genuine ministry by himself. He is not called to such a solo performance. *He is, rather, called to get himself out of the way that Christ might perform through him.* We believe that Christ is the perfect reflection of God. We also hold that God is love. Since Christ in man is the hope of glory, then the church officer will seek above all else to become a channel through which the love of God in Christ can operate for his holy purposes.

When are we worthy of our office? Only when we understand that our first call is a call to be agents of Christ's love. To be leaders toward this end is our sacred responsibility.

4. A fourth principle for the pastoral ministry of church officers remains: *We follow the lead of the Holy Spirit in all our contacts.*

I had a Quaker friend who was fond of saying, "I felt the evil in me weakened and the Spirit of the Lord raised up!" This is our number one aim as church officers.

It might be possible for a church officer to perform his duties faithfully without real love in his heart. He could function out of a stern sense of responsibility. Perhaps his background might be such that he does what he does for selfish reasons. There have been churchmen of this type in many churches and only the

Lord knows whether their efforts have been worthwhile. But, as we have been saying, the single motivating factor worth keeping alive in this service is the holy love of Christ at work through us.

It is well to understand these deeper aspects of our work before we move on toward the surface matters of organization. The "do's and don'ts," the consideration of "what to do when," are secondary items. But to love at all times with a Christian love is more than most of us can manage by ourselves. Yet the genius of our faith is that we are not alone. When we are truly in tune with the Infinite, God brings his Holy Spirit to real life in us.

If we are serious we will study techniques, effective approaches, rules, standards, and human directives. We will want to read and discuss and learn. But the Bible makes it clear that we do not concern ourselves *first* with these things. In clear language it tells us that the Holy Spirit will direct our speech; he will listen through our ears, he will see through our eyes, and he will even pray through our prayers.

It is a good thing that this is true. This book does not attempt to cover all the contingencies which might arise in the pastoral ministry of church officers. Even if that were possible within the pages of one book, it would merit a worthier pen than this author holds in his hand. But because the Indwelling Presence really does come to live in our hearts when we let him, we do not need to sit up nights and worry about what comes next in particular situations.

As you continue your study of this book, will you return often to this chapter and review these four sources or origins? They are the "ultimate basis or cause" of our ministry as shepherds under the Good Shepherd.

The remainder of this book is commentary on Chapter II. It is all right to possess "know-how," "how-to," and the very latest up-to-date information. But these are all toward one holy end— that we may be instruments in God's hands for drawing his own to himself.

III

ORGANIZING FOR
THIS MINISTRY

It would be ideal if every member of the church was so filled with the love of Christ that he had an automatic concern for his fellow members. But many noble resolves soon die away unless there is some built-in development for nudging the will to action.

For this reason an organizational plan of pastoral ministry among Elders and Deacons is a must in most churches.

A good place to start is in officer training.

The alert leader of men knows that a good time to instruct new officers is while they are still new. Those freshly elected to this leadership will generally appreciate some carefully planned period of instruction. In addition to study of the *Book of Church Order*, the *Confession of Faith*, the denominational handbooks for Elders and Deacons, it is wise to include some understanding of each officer's obligations in pastoral ministry. This may come as a surprise to those who have not observed such performance in the local setting. Many churches, as the Board executive says, assume that the preacher is hired to do this work and they have been in the habit of leaving it with him. But a carefully laid-out study of Scripture and ecclesiastical directives will open up new horizons of service to the uninformed.

A wise pastor will make it clear to his leaders that they are invited to share with him the myriad responsibilities of shepherding the flock. He will early invite his officers to keep their minds open and hearts receptive to God's call in this ministry.

One church asks its church officers to make at least one call as a part of their education for leadership. When they report back on the efforts, some have discovered for the first time that they

18

have a real knack for this. One officer said, "I had been thinking of myself for so long I didn't realize the world is full of Johnsons and Smiths with heartaches of their own."

Most churchmen have learned that no plan is one hundred percent effective. Even the most carefully worked-out effort, with follow-up and explicit direction, has never resulted in total efficiency. But leaders who carry out this ministry should not be discouraged by those who neglect their responsibilities. Even Jesus told about one who said he would go but did not. Patience and long-suffering are essentials for anyone dealing with people.

It would seem prudent also to allow for the fact that some men will never be fitted to take part in this program. Certain elected officers are naturally timid. Some have unpleasant memories of thwarted attempts in their previous church experience. Special periods of preparation may be necessary in individual cases. One successful method is to use a lay-expert to train the new recruits. It is sometimes good to assign the hesitant to accompany a successful worker on some of his calls. By observation, the fearful one may be "taught of the Holy Spirit" and by him encouraged to take up the work himself.

Some method of calling assignments must be planned. Whatever the system, the rule seems to be that simplicity should be one stamp of any good method.

Some churches are organized into "parish" or "zone" units with a church officer in charge of each grouping. If such a program is adopted, the key is to keep the responsibility assignments small enough for each officer to do thorough work. One church with a long history in this usage limits each officer to ten families. A map is kept in the church office with each "zone" designated by heavy lines. Colored pins represent the officer's house and the homes in his care. By this means those in charge can see at a glance who to call when a need arises. Any church adopting the system does well to allow for some unassigned Elders and Deacons who can be notified when area leaders are out of town, or preoccupied, or otherwise unable to go when needed.

Other ministers prefer to work directly with their officers on a different basis. They have learned who makes the best sick calls.

They know that certain leaders have a knack for visiting new parents. They trust particular men above others in cases of death. They find it best to assign certain calls to certain officers and experience soon shows who will act promptly and which man fits best in specified assignments. Some men are best suited to "rejoice with those that do rejoice" and others to "weep with those who weep." For this reason the pastor may find it best to channel the entire program through his own office. A good lay-chairman heading up the program may be essential in larger churches. In such cases the leader should be chosen for his overall concept of the church and his ability to attend carefully to details.

Where it can be done, the direct contact between "shepherd" and "under-shepherd" has the advantage of personal discussion with special directions making the call more fruitful. In addition, this method provides a built-in frequent contact point between pastor and officers.

No matter what method is used, it may be well to continue in this ministry those who are rotated off the boards. Some of these may wish to retire temporarily from the work and take it up again later as their service to the church. Elders and Deacons who do not wish to return to the elected leadership may be glad to carry on this ministry even though they are not active on the Session and Diaconate.

The minister, by whatever method adopted, is key man in any plan of pastoral ministry by laymen.

A famous American preacher of another generation is purported to have said, "I never go calling that I do not think about the sermon I should be writing and I never write a sermon without thinking about the calls I should be making." Most ministers know what he means. It takes large blocks of time on the phone and in personal contact with leaders for the minister to direct a successful program of lay contacts. But if he is big enough to see the officer's work as an extention of God's love for his people, he may realize that this is the most valuable time he spends. It also requires humility for him to conceive that other feet and other hands are sometimes as effective or more so, than his own.

Report-backs are important. One highly effective program of church officer ministry is operated almost entirely during the regular monthly meeting time. A period is given early in each session for callers to report their efforts. One man may tell with enthusiasm his success with an inactive family. Another describes his hospital visits and attests to the blessing which came to him from this work. That man outlines his contacts with prospects, and this one recites the joy of a shut-in member who welcomed his prayer for Christ's presence in her loneliness. Failures are described also, and some negative reactions are outlined for the board's information.

After the reports are received, time is given for new assignments. These have been placed on cards prepared prior to the meeting, and names are read with officers volunteering. One will prefer to call on those he knows personally, and another will accept a particular type call which he makes best. It will be readily seen that here again the minister must have spent valuable hours in preparing the list for calling this month. In larger churches, members of the staff may assist him in providing these items for the meeting.

It will be clear that some reports should not wait for the meeting date but ought to be made promptly to the pastor. In certain cases the family visited will need immediate contact from the minister. Other matters should be reported at once to church school leaders, choir members, the office personnel. It is a good day for the program when each participant recognizes that he is only half done after he has made his call. His report-back, either at the regular time, or immediately if the occasion demands, may be necessary to help the church complete its mission.

Only God knows which of his assignments brings the most telling result in the plan of his Kingdom. But any church which develops channels through which his love can flow will find its effort well rewarded. Such a church will also understand the witness of one Elder who said, "I almost had a chip on my shoulder when they asked me to get on this calling program. I thought this was the preacher's job. But after a few months of sharing the ministry I know I'm a better Christian. I also know one family who is still together today because our church was able to meet their needs through my contacts. Can you imagine that? God used *me,* of all people, to save a home. They have new hope and I have new life and I sense a new spirit of love in this old church. I wouldn't take anything for this experience."

This is one of the great facts of our Christian calling. The more we try to do for the Lord and other people, the more we are blessed ourselves.

An anonymous poet puts it well:

I went to see a sick friend,
For years he'd been in bed;
I thought to cheer him up a bit,
But he cheered me instead.

IV

THE MORE SERIOUS CALLS

Home Calls

"They should visit the people at their homes, especially the sick . . ." (*Book of Church Order*, § 11–4).

When illness takes the church officer into the home, the situation may range from a happy recuperative period to that solemn waiting for death which hangs like a pall over the whole household.

If the patient is recovering following an accident, surgery, or long illness, the times of despair and fear are likely giving way to inner songs of thanksgiving and hope for tomorrow. In such cases it may be well to lead into conversations about the future—"It will be great to have you back at church once more!" "We'll be glad to see you on the street again!" "Hope you'll be out in time for the big game." The patient will relish now this pushing back the curtain of tomorrow and the assurance that the world waits on tiptoe for his recovery. The officer does well on these calls to read from such Scriptures as the one hundred and third Psalm:

Bless the LORD, O my soul;
 and all that is within me, bless his holy name!
Bless the LORD, O my soul,
 and forget not all his benefits,
who forgives all your iniquity,
 who heals all your diseases,
who redeems your life from the Pit,
 who crowns you with steadfast love and mercy . . .

A prayer of thanksgiving might properly follow such reading

since the church member coming out of his valley is usually grateful for one of his officers expressing his gratitude in prayer.

On the other hand, if the patient is not likely to recover, he is more prone to enjoy references to the past. Particularly he may be helped with recollections of the days when he was active. If he made some kind of contribution to the life of the church, this is especially good conversational matter on such calls. It will be well for the officer to determine from loved ones or the doctor just how much this person knows of his illness. If he wants to talk about it, the best procedure is to let him express himself. Sometimes it is well to ask, "Have you talked this over with the pastor? He's so understanding about things like this." This could be the very statement needed to give the patient courage for seeking ministerial counsel in his fears.

When death is impending in a family, the caller does well to pray about his ministry to those others in the home who watch and wait. Anything he can do to soften their coming blow will be well received. One officer of our acquaintance spent a half day each Saturday with the sick man for three months to give a harried wife time for shopping, visiting, and just being away from the gloomy setting. Another stopped twice weekly for several weeks with a quart of ice cream for his dying friend.

Books checked out of the church library may be welcomed by those on the way up or on the way down. Visits from others in the church, prompted by the officer, may add much to the waiting period.

Times of Sorrow

"It belongs to their office . . . to . . . comfort the mourner . . ." (*Book of Church Order,* § 11–4).

At no time is the visitor from the church more welcome in a home than when death strikes. But the rule generally is, "The less you say the better." Some well-meaning souls feel that they must give an oration or at least say something impressive. Usually, the fact that you have come is enough, and a firm handclasp or a pat on the back is likely to be more appreciated than flowery words. "Bear up, Sophie!" may make you feel that you have at least said something, but she may feel like screaming if one more cliché comes her way. It is well to let her know you stand ready to help. You might ask her what small thing you could do for her, and then, unless you are almost next of kin, you will probably help most if you excuse yourself and leave. You may wish to have a prayer with the folks who have gathered. If you do, it should be a prayer of thanksgiving for the one gone on, for God's presence there in the room right now, and for the Christian's faith that life is eternal. Follow-up in such cases is top priority. Especially is this true as the days pass and the rest of the well-wishers have dwindled away.

Special Emergencies

"It is the duty of the Deacons, first of all, to minister to . . . any who may be in distress" (*Book of Church Order*, § 12–3).

When bad tidings come to the home, or a divorce threatens, or a child gets into trouble, or there is an accident, or fire strikes, or the business fails—when calamity of any kind strikes a sudden blow—the rule here is: "As soon as you hear it, drop everything and go!" As one lady put it, "I thought maybe the whole world was breaking up! Then you came. Your calm presence settled my nerves and I could see what I had to do."

If hysteria has taken firm hold and there is no way to settle the panic, it is well to call a doctor, or the minister, or some other professional who has seen this sort of thing before.

Calls on the unemployed fit into this category. The best thing one can do at such times is to aid in every possible way toward re-employment. Many times fellow officers can assist with a clue which is productive. On such calls as this the member may refer to his embarrassment at not being able to carry out his church pledge. A safe rule is to make no mention of this unless the subject is opened by the person visited. Then it should be set in its proper perspective with assurance that this is not the church's first concern. If the church has strong emphasis on percentage giving, this will be easier. Ten percent of nothing is nothing, and the Lord knows the true condition of every life.

Prison calls are another special emergency of the most dramatic kind. In even the best-run churches there may come days when embezzlement, tax evasion, and other serious charges have brought a fellow member behind bars. Here is a very specialized ministry which may not open to some officers in an entire lifetime.

If the imprisonment is for an extended period, your major contribution is most likely to be with those whose family flag has been lowered to half-mast. They need encouragement. They need assurance that the church will love them no matter what comes.

If it should fall your lot to call at the jail, you would do well to consult your pastor first, or, better still, the prison chaplain who has been many times along these cold, gray corridors. He will advise you what to say and what to leave unsaid.

You will of course leave all "judgment" to the courts and school yourself ahead of time in the mercy of God and his endless love for all who have sinned including you yourself.

Calls Where Alcoholics Are Involved

One of the most serious social problems of our generation centers in the problem drinkers. Authorities tell us that there are several million of these in our country and the number is increasing. It is probable that the church caller will eventually be confronted with this problem in his visiting.

A good place to start is for the caller to acquaint himself with Alcoholics Anonymous and other organizations set up to work well with these unfortunate people. "AA" has grown to such an extent that most communities either have a group of their own or have one within driving distance. In some major cities there is a national organization known as the "Council on Alcoholism" which can give excellent advice and provide study materials. These "Councils" work closely with Alcoholics Anonymous. They are glad to provide a list of meeting places. They may welcome the opportunity to give programs to church groups. So extensive is this problem that most families either have someone in their circle of relatives who needs this type of help, or are acquainted with people who are in the throes of this struggle.

If the caller is interested in depth study on this subject, there are several excellent books available. One of the best in this author's acquaintance is Howard Clinebell's *Understanding and Counseling the Alcoholic,* published by Abingdon Press in 1956. Another worthy writing is Marty Mann's *New Primer on Alcoholism,* published by Holt, Rinehart & Winston in 1958. It would be impossible here to set down a full record of guidepoints, but there are a few major items worth remembering:

A. The best thing which the amateur can do for the alcoholic and his family is to refer them to those who are experienced. This problem is likely to be beyond the range of the average church caller's ability to handle by himself.

B. Alcoholism is a sickness. This is a very important concept and one which is difficult for the average layman to grasp. It needs diligent study from authoritative sources before it can be fully understood. The caller should aim to be as patient and encouraging, as wise and guarded in his conversation, as he would be in the case of grave illnesses which are more natural to his experience.

C. The alcoholic cannot be helped until he is ready to confess that he is in need of help. He cannot be pushed, or shamed, or coerced into taking this first step toward recovery. The church caller would do well to let him know that help is available when he is ready. But the officer should be wary of well-meaning relatives who urge someone from the church to "talk to him" or "see if you can straighten him out."

D. The church caller can probably do his best work here in his ministry to the family of alcoholics. There is scarcely any problem which produces more soul-agony for a distraught husband or wife. The caller does well to ask himself, "What would I like someone to do for me if I had this heartache?" The Golden Rule is a solid operating principle for work with alcoholics and their loved ones.

E. Consultation with the pastor is very much in order following visits to the homes of problem drinkers. In most cases the minister will probably be acquainted with this situation. There is always the possibility, however, that he may be unaware of the problem. In most cases, church callers would do well to check their efforts here with the minister.

Mental Illness

Here, too, the church officer does well to step aside in favor of the more experienced as soon as he recognizes that he is over his head. There is a well-put definition of the difference between a psychotic and a neurotic. This bit of doggerel may be helpful at this point: "A psychotic is one who thinks that two and two are five. A neurotic is one who knows that two and two are four but it makes him nervous."

Whenever the flock-member just doesn't make sense in his reasoning, there is strong likelihood that the church officer is in water too deep for the layman. If the member puts two things together and they come out beyond the pale of what any clear thinker would know—if they add this to that and get something quite preposterous—it is well to talk this one over with the pastor and let him have a look at the situation. When an officer comes on an emotional roller coaster flying to abnormal heights and then plunging to unprecedented depths, unless he is a professional he will know that someone other than himself should find the switch to stop this terror. This is particularly so if the ups and downs are coming with increasing frequency and intensity.

Two apparently contradictory indications are also an occasion for serious consideration. One of these is when the patient talks incessantly about a particular subject, running the record over and over. The other is when there is no continuity to the conversation. The train of thought goes off its track now to run all over the field without heading in the general direction of any depot. Both of these signs often indicate that there is serious trouble ahead.

Hate of such intensity that it can't quit waving the red flag of bitterness may also indicate serious trouble ahead.

Wherever there is any doubt, the church leader does well to bow out quickly and call someone who knows his way through these shadows. He is wise whose major ministry to mental and emotional illness consists chiefly of earnest prayer for the sick mind and concern for the family involved. Or it goes best when the patient has recovered and needs assurance that he is still welcome in his former circles.

"Blessed is the church officer who remembers his amateur standing!"

Hospital Calls

These deserve a chapter of their own, but since they too are of the more serious variety we will consider them here.

After determining the patient's condition from the family, it is important to inquire at the hospital for visiting hours. Then, on reaching the floor, it is proper for the officer to request special permission. Almost any nurse responds favorably to the statement, "I am calling for my church, and I would like to see him if it will be all right for me to visit."

Some points to remember about hospital calling:

It is a good idea to sit down and relax for a moment in the nearest chair unless the patient is too sick to visit. Hospital calls should be shorter than any other visits, but don't let the patient think you are rushing! There is enough intensity in the hospital room without your adding to it by nervous demeanor. If you do sit down, don't make like a ramrod. Let yourself go back as though at least one person still feels at home in the universe. The patient is not at home and he doesn't feel at home. It will help him if you do. I learned this from a wise doctor.

In one parish where I served as pastor there were two doctors who had offices together, and they often saw each other's patients. One of them was in the habit of dashing into the room, poking about hurriedly, and rushing off to his next patient. People often complained that he seemed preoccupied. The other doctor would come in, make his examination as though he had all the time in the world; then he would sit down for a few seconds, cross his legs, and give the impression that he was set for a long visit. This second doctor, who was an officer in our church, loved to laugh about it as he said, "The truth is I don't stay any longer than my partner. But the patient thinks I do because I sit down." Then he would advise me, "I know you're a busy pastor, but for goodness' sake don't ever let anyone think you are hurrying with his problems. He will secretly hate you for it, and you can never be a blessing in a rush."

I am glad to pass this on as sage advice from a wise physician whose healing was much more thorough than mere medicine could provide.

Instead of asking the patient, "How are you feeling?" it will be better if you phrase your question, "How is it going?"

I learned this from one of America's best-known hospital chaplains when I was in seminary. Whenever I have forgotten it, the lag has been to my sorrow and sometimes to the embarrassment of the patient. If you ask the first question and he is not feeling well, he may prefer to lie, which couldn't add to his inner well-being. Or he may put you down with all the other run-of-the-mill comers whom he is glad to see leave and he doesn't know why. "How is it going?" can also be answered with fewer words and from the top of his head without beating the weary mental path once again to his true aches and pains.

If the patient is in grave condition and he knows it, he may allude to death with some such statement as, "I don't think I'm going to make it!"

Now all the angels in heaven bend low to hear what you will answer. The same chaplain, above referred to, taught us that the proper answer is, "Well, everything will be all right anyway, won't it?" I have used this phrase many times, and I have had people who later recovered thank me for my wisdom (which obviously wasn't mine) and for giving them something to think about when I left the room. Some have told me that even if they were not sure death would be all right with them it did help them to know that I was this confident. Then those who can muster the courage to say, "Yes, it's all right!" may be expressing for the first time their own forgotten faith that life is eternal and that God is greater than death.

If someone in your charge is in "the valley of the shadow of death" you will do well to acquaint yourself with Scriptures and center your bedside prayers in words greater than your own from God's own Word.

Prayer in the hospital room is usually very much welcomed.
It will be appreciated if your thoughts before God are well
chosen. They should be because they have a way of leaving their
tracks on the soul of this sick one. Should there be other patients
in the room, if they are awake, or if they appear to be asleep,
your prayers should include them. Any minister could tell you of
miracles of God's grace which reached out and touched pre-
viously untouched lives through prayer in the sickroom. In certain other situations of pastoral ministry, the rule may be, "If
you're in doubt, don't!" But with prayer in the sickroom the better rule is, "If you're in doubt, do!"

I have also found on numerous occasions that the prayer of a
layman said at a bedside has a much more telling impact than the
prayer of a clergyman. People expect the minister to pray, but
when a fellow church member prays this seems to plumb depths
unreachable by the man of the cloth.

The Sudden Sickness

A heart attack, an accident, a quick shutdown of life at its
normal pace, is sure to happen sometime in even the smallest
group assigned to the church officer. This is a humbling experience, especially for the man who has fallen into the habit of
thinking the world cannot get on without him. If all his life he
has demanded top billing, this will be almost too much to bear.
The wealthy man, accustomed to seeing doors fly open at the
sight of his money, faces a drastic inner adjustment when he
comes to that spot where his dollars can't buy his way back to the
office immediately.

This particular ministry requires the most sensitive of officers.
He should be one whose loving heart is even more eloquent than
the words of his lips. We have found it especially good at times
like this to appoint some church officer who has walked this particular dreary road himself. In any gathering of churchmen there
is likely to be someone who has been there before no matter how
severe the case. It is good to use these men to witness not from
"What I would do" but "What I did when I was where you are."
This officer might well be one who is able to pray with the

stricken. This is a good rule for all callers: The graver the case, the surer the power of prayer to help and strengthen.

The Eternal "Why?"

Anyone who works with people at their calamity points will sooner or later come headlong into this question. "Why should God do this to me?"—"I don't understand why this had to happen to us!"—"We have tried to be good and it doesn't seem fair!"—are common dirges in the sickroom.

It will be readily sensed by anyone who has been there that such questions are but futile hammering at doors which never can be opened. Men have been picking at this lock for generations, and no one has ever opened all the doors in this dark castle. The only honest answer is that there isn't any answer unless we side-step the direct question and come at it from a different vantage point.

Even some "good" church members in their adversity will be pounding their fists on the table and demanding that God do what is "right" by his own. They have secretly believed in the Heavenly Father as a baby sitter for their own private interests.

For such as these it may require a whole new course in theology before they can be comforted. Perhaps this treatment may call for a ministry beyond the church officer's best efforts.

But anyone who has settled the matter in his own heart can attest that faith is not a celestial insurance policy with some cosmic casualty company. The Bible never promises exemption from dark and fearsome valleys. It only assures that the Good Shepherd will be with us through these valleys! And when we pray with these "Why-Oh-Why?" people, we can somehow hope they will observe that prayer is not for getting God into a corner where he must do what we ask. Real prayer is God bringing us into a place where we listen for his direction and are willing to do as he asks. Pure prayer is not God on his knees before man: it is man on his knees to be taught of God.

So perhaps our best witness is to understand prayer like this and be able to relate it to others in this spirit. And we can testify too that even though they are at the end of their rope God never gets to the end of his rope. We poor frail people may be smaller than the things which happen to us but the Sovereign God is bigger than anything which happens. Ever and eternally he knows and cares and can use life's tragedies in his plan. If we keep faith and keep open our hearts, we may yet sing his song in this strange land.

V

SOME OTHER VISITS

Calls on the Shut-ins

"It's been a long time between drinks!" This was the comical greeting of one of my favorite shut-ins. She was letting me know that I called too seldom to keep her contented. But some shut-ins are that way, and even if the church called every week on people of this ilk they would wonder why we didn't come daily.

A sense of humor is good equipment to take along on visits to the old folks or those who are in for the rest of their lives. They may be bitter, and it is well to put ourselves in their place and think how we would feel if we never heard the birds firsthand or shared in the daily "busyness" of the market place.

Regularity is one thing needful with these calls and encouragement is another. You should have a good answer too for that chronic "the preacher never comes" complaint. You might preclude these arrows with the shield of tolerance for the busy shepherd. It is well to explain that you are here in the pastor's stead. Then, if the time is getting unbearable, whisper in his ear that "Grandma" is lonely for her pastor.

Shut-ins love to talk about their families, and you will hit the mark with them if you ask to see the grandchildren's pictures which they just might have handy. You'll be sure to thank them also for their contribution to church-life in days gone by. If your church has an intercessory praying ministry, they'll be proud to share this pastoral responsibility, and you should make arrangements for them to add their name to this all-important service. Nothing is quite so desolate as to be relegated to the shelf with no sense of mission any more. Maybe they could address letters for the church office, or make phone calls on special occasions, or in some other way feel that their membership still had some service potential.

Prayer with shut-ins is usually much appreciated and Scripture reading also is well received. Most pastors will be glad to provide their laymen with suggestions, but helpful verses may be selected from Psalm 23, Psalm 46, Isaiah 40, John 14, Matthew 5, Romans 8, 1 Corinthians 12-13.

The Complainers

This district-attorney type is part of the scenery in any congregation. They are usually full of charges and counter-charges. Some folks only feel good when they feel bad, and maybe you'd rather take a beating than go back for more of their vitriol. But of one thing you can be sure—your pastor will be ever grateful to you for letting them pound your ear rather than his. If these fall your lot, you do well to go with your mind centered in such Scriptures as Philippians 4:8—"whatever is true, whatever is honorable, whatever is just, whatever is pure, whatever is lovely, whatever is gracious, if there is any excellence, if there is anything worthy of praise, think about these things." With thoughts like these tucked away in your mind you can ponder them in depth as the complainers get out their hammers and pound away.

There is another type of complainer which you do well to consider more seriously. These are the nice people with new gripes about which something can be done. These might well be reported to the officers, or to the pastor, or both. Sometimes if the burr is new under the saddle it can be removed before it results in a permanent sore. You will pray for the wisdom of Solomon that you may distinguish the real from the chronic. Sometimes these things, if passed on, would only cause undue consternation for pastor and other leaders. Sometimes you do all that is needed when you only listen and let them get it off their chests. If you don't pray with them, you will pray for them, and for wisdom to separate the wheat from the chaff before carrying it further. These people of the personality like a dental drill are not easy. But they are God's children, and they too are a part of the Household of Faith.

The Radicals

After an evening spent with these you may wonder why the lions were not thrown to the Christians instead of vice versa. They may seem like a new phenomenon on the horizon, but a careful study of Scripture will reveal that the early church also had some of these "My mind is made up, don't confuse me with the facts" people.

They may be race-baiters, or poor frightened souls who look under the bed each night to be sure there isn't a Communist lurking there, or superpatriots who believe in freedom only for those who believe as they do. To get into an argument with these is to create a spawning place for greater discord in the church. Unless you join them one hundred percent in their prowl for evildoers you cannot possibly hope to appease them.

If you should be so unfortunate as to have them on your responsibility list, you will report their presence to the proper authorities, and you will pray that one day they may come to know the love of God as they apparently do not know it now.

Some of these people are church-hoppers who come into a congregation certain that their newfound minister is the greatest they have ever heard. But given enough time they will doubtless move on when another minister comes to the church around the corner. They will then be sure that he is the prophet Jeremiah reincarnate or one of the Apostles—but only for a time.

My mother used to say that there are two kinds of funny. There is "funny ha-ha" and then there is "funny peculiar." These people are "funny peculiar." They need what love we can get through to them and they need our prayers. But they do not merit our getting upset. The Master of men saw some folks go away too. It's like my godly depot-agent Elder in Nebraska told me once: "When you've done all you can, quit stewing, boy! Jesus lost one out of twelve and comparing you with Jesus you'd do well to hold one out of twelve."

There is a fine line between a hard heart and the philosophical acceptance of our limitations. Happy are we when we find it.

The Happy Calls

The arrival of a new baby is a good time for pastoral ministry. Parents are open to God's touch at this time in a special way. Perhaps it is because their little one is so fresh from God and they sense somehow that anything as wonderful as this must have divine origin. This is another place where the prayer of the church officer will be gratefully received. It would be appropriate also to discuss baptism and its meaning with the young parents.

Marriage is another occasion when special attention is welcomed, provided, of course, that it isn't too close to the wedding date when everyone in the household is already frazzled with myriad matters. The parents of the bride and groom will be glad for your coming when the ceremony is over and still fresh in their minds. They love to run it over again, to show you the pictures, and to hear you tell what a beautiful wedding it was. The bride and groom will more likely prefer your letter of congratulations to a personal visit. Later on, you, and they, may find it good to have a call in their newly established home. Once again "prayer is wont to be made" in such a setting.

Success is another item which should not go unnoticed by the church. The doctor opens a new hospital, the rising young executive receives another promotion, a daughter graduates with honors, the contractor starts his big building, Bruiser is named to the all-state team, or any one of many other high points is reached. The alert church officer knows in such cases that he can bring this family closer to the church by offering his congratulations in person or by letter.

Children

Some undershepherds are especially cut out for work with the lambs of the flock. When a child is recovering, it is well to remember: (a) "A cheerful heart is a good medicine . . ." (Prov. 17:22). Children need a smile and a laugh and a gay countenance. (b) They are especially helped by some small gift—a children's book, a red apple, a bright-colored toy. (c) This little life may be "won" to the Lord, if not now, at some later date in the memory of "that nice man from the church who came to see me when I was sick." (d) Parents are often more deeply touched and grateful for something done for their children than for themselves. This ministry to "the wee ones" is one of the most vital impacts which the church can make.

Other Opportunities for Pastoral Contact

When a son arrives on furlough from the armed forces, when a family goes abroad, when the first child leaves home for college, or any other occasion when the household is swept to emotional heights, this is a time when folks are receptive to special attention. A positive impact may be made for the church which lets folks know that Christ cares about everything which happens in their lives. The wise officer will sense whether he should go, or would a well-timed phone call be more appreciated? By whatever method he decides is right, he can use this moment to seal the family to the Household of Faith and make the church a blessing to these hearts.

The Ministry of Correspondence

One officer of my acquaintance kept up correspondence with more than fifty men of his church who were away at war. Another sends a quarterly letter from his office to every student of the church away at school. This church takes credit for a fine summer program with its college youth but this is no accident. One girl wrote, "How could I tell you what it means to get that letter every quarter with the devotional guide?" A bright young man who is considering the ministry as his life work says, "In three months I'm kind of running out of the good stuff in me. Then comes that letter. It jerks me up and sets me straight again."

Neither of these men felt useful as callers. But by dedicated pen and committed typewriter they have been a vital part of the pastoral ministry of church officers in their church.

In one church when people move from the parish they are included in the cards distributed at meetings of the boards. Each officer who takes one of these is asked to write a letter of appreciation to the departed members for their contribution to the church. They urge these folks to find a new church home quickly. They take this means of letting their fellow Christians know that the church cares not only when they are new members, but when they leave they are also precious to the heart of the Lord.

When we put our ear down close to the New Testament we hear certain unmistakable sounds in the life of the church—these are the quiet steps of Christians making their way to the homes of their fellow members—the tapping of dedicated knuckles at doors which need his ministry—the laughter and weeping and conversation from hearts possessed by the indwelling Christ who loves and cares. When we give ourselves to this work, we take our place in a long chain of love, and it dawns on us that his continuing ministry is the one great need and the one great hope for his Kingdom to come on earth.

VI

CALLS CONCERNING
CHURCH MEMBERSHIP

An old proverb says, "Most footprints on the sands of time were made with work shoes." This is a message for contemporary churches. If we are to leave a lasting mark on our world, there will likely be some well-worn shoe leather on the soles of our feet.

We turn now to certain calls dealing with church membership.

Calling on Church Transfers

Rule worth remembering: The sooner the officer arrives after the prospect moves into his new home, the better the impression he makes for his church. Every day he dallies is time lost. The newcomer may be moved to positive reaction if "the church" cares enough to seek him out quickly. If this is neglected he may gradually drift off into the legions of those whose only claim to membership is that they know which church they are staying away from.

Whenever he goes, his main emotion should be one of enthusiasm. "You don't want to buy any can openers, do you?" does not sell can openers, and this same lack of fervor can be deadly doing for the church. Always for any product a green salesman gets more orders than a blue one. One mark of the New Testament Christian was his excitement. It should be the same with us.

On these calls the church officer does well to acquaint himself thoroughly with the exact procedure for transferring membership. He must know well the time, the method, and all involvements connected with the transfer of a church letter. Again, when some question is asked which he cannot answer, he will admit his lack of knowledge and follow it up with a phone call, note, or personal visit when he relays what he has learned from right sources. No one expects anyone to know everything and this attention to needs is likely to be much appreciated by the newcomer.

Evangelism Calls on the Non-Christian

The officer who makes these calls will be much in the spirit of that little four-word prayer: "Lord, speak through me!"

Officers who make evangelistic contacts on the unchurched should be steeped in the love of God. Some church leaders are possessed of a theology which gives free expression to the thought that there is a hot hell-fire waiting for the unconverted. There may be, but few in this author's experience have been frightened into a lasting relationship with God.

The Bible tells us that one fruit of the Spirit is gentleness and another is patience (Gal. 5:22-23). The most effective lay-evangelists I have known were marked by these traits. "God is love" seemed to be their theme-text. They invariably were more effective with their message of the Waiting Father of Luke 15 than those with fire in their eyes whose major note was "the wages of sin is death"! This latter verse is equally as real as the former reference, but in my experience more people have been drawn to the heart of God by a loving Savior than have been driven home by the concept of a wrathful judge.

When one discusses salvation with the unsaved, he does well to have a clear outline in his own mind which he can transfer in lucid terms from his own head and heart to the heart of his hearer.

Here is a suggested statement of the steps in God's plan of salvation.

I

GOD MADE US AND WE ARE HIS—

"You are not your own; you were bought with a price. So glorify God in your body."

1 Corinthians 6:19-20

II

GOD SENT JESUS CHRIST TO SHOW US WHAT HE (GOD) IS LIKE AND TO SHOW US WHAT WE (MAN) OUGHT TO BE—

"He who has seen me has seen the Father . . ."

John 14:9

". . . Christ also suffered for you, leaving you an example, that you should follow in his steps."

1 Peter 2:21

III

BUT EVERY ONE OF US HAS SINNED. BECAUSE GOD GAVE US FREE WILL WE HAVE ALL CHOSEN OUR WAY RATHER THAN GOD'S WAY. THIS IS SIN—

". . . all have sinned and fall short of the glory of God . . ."

Romans 3:23

"If we say we have no sin, we deceive ourselves, and the truth is not in us."

1 John 1:8

IV

JESUS CHRIST BY HIS ATONING DEATH HAS THE POWER TO RESTORE US TO PERFECT FELLOWSHIP WITH GOD—THIS IS WHAT ATONEMENT MEANS— "AT-ONE-MEANT"—WE WERE MEANT TO BE AT ONE WITH GOD AND THROUGH CHRIST THIS BECOMES POSSIBLE—

"For God has not destined us for wrath, but to obtain salvation through our Lord Jesus Christ, who died for us . . ."

1 Thessalonians 5:9–10

"All this is from God, who through Christ reconciled us to himself . . ."

2 Corinthians 5:18

V

THIS SALVATION TAKES PLACE WHEN WE INVITE THE RISEN CHRIST INTO OUR HEARTS TO BE THE LORD AND RULER OF OUR LIVES—

"Behold, I stand at the door, and knock; if any one hears my voice and opens the door, I will come in to him and eat with him, and he with me."

Revelation 3:20

". . . Christ in you, the hope of glory."

Colossians 1:27

It will be understood that this is not an attempt to cover all Christian theology in one brief statement. But the church officer will do well to study some such outline, adding his own scriptural insight, until he can put in his own words the gospel of God's redeeming grace in Christ Jesus. (He may be wise to consult his pastor and work out some other simple presentation consistent with the preaching from the pulpit of his church.)

It is a wise man who knows his limitations, and there will be some good officers who can never make this type of call with success. There are some truly saved souls who cannot describe their experience in words. If a man is not cut out for this, he can simply confess that this requires a more certain sound than that of his poor trumpet. Such an honest saint will do the church a blessing if he states his inadequacy and turns this over to one with words to match the moment.

Blessed is the church officer who does not speak glibly beyond his own experience and ability!

Calls on the Inactive Member

Working with those who have lost interest may be one of the toughest assignments in the pastoral ministry of church officers. The seeds which sprang up quickly have withered now. If at all possible, this growth must be revived.

The main matter is to get there quickly when the flower begins to fade. Too often we let it dry up until even the most thorough waterings cannot bring it back.

If we do make it in time, we may find some bug which has been gnawing at the roots and needs our attention. Grievances are of diverse kinds. It may be hurt feelings which were innocently trampled, or maybe not so innocently. Some folks came into the church with the mistaken concept that this was chiefly to do something for them. They were not told that the church exists as a place where they can do something for Christ. Or maybe they weren't listening. It may require a whole new concept of "the church" before they can be brought back into the fellowship of service.

Perchance the pastor didn't call often enough, and they felt that he didn't care. Maybe the officer's major contribution will be to give them a new understanding of the ministry. Or perhaps a word in the pastor's ear will be all that is required for helping them over this hurdle.

One place to look (very carefully and with a deft touch) is in their pocketbook. Some people don't like "statements," or they got behind in their pledge, or they are ultra-sensitive at this point. They may need to discuss at length the Christian idea of stewardship as a regular, systematic, covenant relationship whereby God is not demanding from them anything more than an open channel whereby he might flow into their lives with all his blessings and through them to all the world.

It will be obvious that this is rough going and requires much of the rare quality of "people-patience."

If, in the officer's best judgment, this case is closed, his duty may be to speak the truth in love. Then he may recommend that they earnestly seek another church where they can be happy and of service to the Lord who loves other denominations as much as our own.

Repeat: The inactive member requires active attention and the sooner the better!

VII

SEVEN "DO'S" AND SEVEN "DON'TS" FOR CHURCH CALLERS

The reader who has come this far will recognize that church calling cannot be by script. We do well to learn the best methods. We should study what the experts in public relations have to say. Most of us find, on close examination, that we do have habits which need correcting. We may have been making obvious mistakes because we were not up on the latest. But to follow rules and apply techniques is not the purpose of church calling. We are representatives of One who fought hard against legalistic living. As we have seen, for him, the "person" was more important than the protocol. Going in his Spirit is our best insurance that we will not make too many damaging mistakes. Walking in his steps we tread safely. As we let him speak through us, his love covers many an error and brings this work to success.

As we listen to the precepts of those who know the finer points, we will also remember that no human knows exactly what will happen when other humans are involved. Some things "ordinarily" take place when touched by certain stimuli. But that "What-in-heaven's-name-do-I-do-now?" feeling, and the "They-never-told-us-about-this-one!" is sure to come sooner or later. Some visits require fast thinking when the "ordinary" does not come off.

Three little rules which have been helpful to some in such moments are:

1. My best preparation is to "go in the Spirit" and accept the Scripture's promise that he will speak through me if I let him. I will go in prayer and be prayerful when the unusual happens.

2. I will be honest. When I don't know I will say so. I can be concerned in Christian love even if I don't have all the answers.

3. Listen! Maybe God's best tools right now are my ears.

Lincoln is purported to have said, "Since God made man with two ears and only one mouth, He must want us to listen twice as much as we talk." Most of us are obviously out of balance much of the time by this formula. Yet here again, the danger of following "rules" is clear. Sometimes we should *not* listen. It is just as bad to listen when we should be speaking as it is to speak when we should be listening. The Bible tells us clearly, "To make an apt answer is a joy to a man, and a word in season, how good it is!" (Prov. 15:23).

So here we go again—church calling, when we do it strictly on our own, may quickly run afoul and have no real merit. Our only hope is to be servants of the Lord whose love is greater than our love and in whose wisdom are all the answers.

For this reason, all references in Chapters IV, V, VI, and VII will best be understood in the light of Chapter II. It might be well right here for the reader to review the "Principles" involved and write again on his heart the words concerning the guidance of the Holy Spirit in every church call.

With this background we present now some "do's" and "don'ts" which have been widely used in our denomination and by our Baptist friends. They were written for church callers by the author and Dr. Ralph Langley, pastor of the Willow Meadows Baptist Church of Houston, Texas. Some workers have found them helpful as adjuncts to the deeper preparation of the Holy Spirit. (They are presented here in revised form.)

SEVEN "DO'S" FOR CHURCH CALLERS

I. *Pray.* The number one "be" for all church visitors is "be prayerful." Before you knock or ring the bell, pray this four-word prayer, "Lord, speak through me!" The Bible promises that he will do this—". . . for what you are to say will be given to you in that hour" (Matt. 10:19). You are representing Christ in this home. This call is for glorifying God by Christ's contact through your contact. If he really is "in you" others will feel his presence in this call. Pray that you may represent him and his church as he wishes. Go in prayer. Visit prayerfully. Go home praying that the Lord will use your efforts. If you are led, you may wish to close this call with prayer. It is often effective to join hands if you do. This closing prayer is not necessary. Do what comes naturally for you and what he leads you to do. Your whole call should be centered in the living prayer, "Lord, speak through me!"

II. *Introductions Are Important!* "What do we say first?" How about "Hello! I'm Bob B. from the church. I came to thank you for visiting us," or "to welcome you!" (Of course you will introduce your partner if you are calling as a team.) You have done three things here. (1) You've told them who you are; (2) you've told them where you're from; (3) you've set the call on a positive note. Remember that the sweetest sound in all the world to the other fellow is his own name. Next comes the names of those he loves. Unless these folks look unusually crisp, you might ask them their first names and repeat yours. In many cases this will contribute to a warm climate for the call.

III. *Listen More Than You Talk.* As soon as you are inside and the introductions are over, get the occupant talking about himself, his family, his job, his ideas. To begin with, he's sure to be more interested in himself than in you or the church. That can come later. Never crush the prospect with yourself or the church. Your words may have the ring of a bell to you, but they will sound like the caw of a crow to him if he is anxiously waiting to express himself. Put out your radar and search for his deeper thoughts. The person who benefits us most is not the one who first tells us something he is thinking. The real "minister" is first of all one who lets us give expression to the truth within us which has been dumbly struggling for utterance. The rest of your call will be more successful if you can get him to express himself first.

IV. *Know Your Church and Guide the Conversation to It.*

You'll make a better impression if you can answer his questions. You have probably attended the church's instruction course for members. If not, you will want to do so at once. Acquaint yourself with questions which might be asked. Read books on your denomination and inform yourself of scheduled activities in the local congregation. What is the date of the men's meeting? When do they baptize babies? What are the church's major beliefs? What is distinctive about our denomination? If you cannot answer promptly, say so, and in cases where the interest warrants get the information and relay it back to the questioner while his question is still fresh. Remember you are calling for the church. It is all right to talk about the game, politics, city affairs, and community matters, but be sure you let this person know you are on a church visit. Find out how you can assist him to a closer relationship with Christ and the Kingdom.

V. *Keep Alert to Special Needs*. How can the church help this family? Do they have a lonesome teen-ager? You and your church can do something about this. Is there some hidden resentment which needs expression? If you are alert, you may sense some conversational trial balloon which the speaker is sending up hoping you will notice. If there is little enthusiasm for the church and its work, witness to what you like about it and why you think it would be a blessing for him. It goes without elaboration that if you don't have a certain fervor, you would not be calling. So if you feel it, go ahead and effervesce. "Let the redeemed of the Lord say so . . ." (Ps. 107:2).

VI. *Leave While They Still Want You to Stay*. Proverbs 25:17 (K.J.V.) offers good advice when it says, "Withdraw thy foot from thy neighbour's house; lest he be weary of thee, and so hate thee." Preachers have been taught (God forbid that we may have forgotten) that it is good to end sermons while the congregation is still interested in hearing more. The same goes for visits in the home. There are some times when the occasion will call for settling back and going deep. Perhaps this person may need a long discussion of his faith. He may have burdens which require an extended unloading. But these are the exception rather than the rule. Generally it is better to err on the side of too short a visit rather than too long. End on the high level of church-concern such as prayer for the family or with an expression of gratitude for their place in the congregation's life, for their time, and of course for their hospitality.

VII. *Your Call Is Not Complete Till You Report Back.* Some visits are not complete in themselves. There may be certain matters which would require follow-up. Maybe you'll need to contact someone else in the church to see about getting the mother in a circle or to provide attention for an aging grandmother who is lonesome. Then too, be sure you note the pertinent facts so that you can report them to your fellow officers at their next meeting, or to the pastor. If you are to send in your report, remember it will not do its full work on top of your dresser. Get it in the mail today! Reporting may be as important as the call and what good you have done could be wiped out if you neglect to follow up.

SEVEN "DON'TS" ON MINOR MATTERS

I. *Don't Sit Where You Will Be Constantly Turning Your Head.* Eye-range is of real importance to an effective call, when you are visiting more than one person. If you possibly can do so, avoid a "split situation" where the wife is on one side of the room and the husband on the other. Try to get both husband and wife within eye-range. You might accomplish this by saying, "Let me sit over here where I can see you both."

II. *Don't Forget to Be Appreciative.* It is still true that "A word fitly spoken is like apples of gold in a setting of silver" (Prov. 25:11). Don't act as though there were a filter on your lips preventing the passage of a kind word. A chattery flattery is not Christian, but if you can't find something worth praising in this family there could be a flaw in your relationship to Christ. You can create a positive climate by observing this Christian grace in an honest way.

III. *Don't Gossip.* "I wouldn't say anything about them unless I could say something good—but, boy, is this good!" Almost everyone tends to gossip sometimes. Whenever this dragon raises its ugly head, change the subject, sidestep the matter, or say something good about X and let it go at that. Even the Apostle Paul had his problems with those "gadding about from house to house, and not only idlers but gossips and busybodies, saying what they should not" (1 Tim. 5:13). Negative talk which begins with "They say," "I heard," or "There is a rumor" has little place in an official visit from the church.

IV. *Don't Argue.* So the church does have faults. It is true that the preacher is not perfect. If this person wants to fuss about hypocrites, socialism, money, doctrines, social issues, or anything —then chances are good you won't advance the Kingdom one bit by joining the anvil chorus. If you think it is doing him good to ventilate his feelings, listen prayerfully. Be tactful, but when the situation is hopeless let the Holy Spirit guide you out the door as gracefully as possible. Fortunately this sort of thing does not happen often, but when it does, your best reaction is the warm love of Christ ruling in your heart.

V. *Don't Stay Home Because the Weather Is Bad.* There is an old adage worth remembering: "The worse the weather, the warmer the welcome." Don't let the storm scare you away. You'll be more likely to find these people (a) at home, (b) anxious to get you in out of the weather, (c) feeling good that they can offer you shelter, (d) impressed that you care enough about your church and their family to come out tonight.

VI. *Don't Let the Phone Question Bother You.* Are prearranged calls better than drop-ins? A good rule to remember here is the Golden Rule. How do you like folks to come to your house? If you phone once, and they are busy, then you will be wise to say, "Of course I understand. How would it be if I just drop in some time?" Chances are good they'll answer, "Fine!" Now you have this on a healthy basis. They'll be expecting you, and you'll feel free about your call.

VII. *Don't Let the Television Destroy Your Call.* This is a tough one which our forebears never had to face. But our age does, and it is well to consider it ahead of time. If the children are watching with enthusiasm, you might suggest to the parents, "Couldn't we sit in the den so as not to disturb the young folks?" If the parents are "glued" to the picture too, you could ask, "Is that your favorite program?" It almost never is, and most folks wouldn't admit it even if it might be. If you must sit in the same room with this one-eyed monster, by all means suggest that you visit over here in the corner while the small fry view on. For permanent effectiveness, it is not good to alienate the children. If you arrive during an exciting game and dad is an avid fan, you may want to watch it with him. Perhaps, if you have another call to make nearby, you could suggest that you come back when the program is over. With this tricky problem, like so many other things, you will need to be at your prayerful best. God will guide you right down to the minor matters if you let him. The Bible admonishes us clearly, ". . . whatever you do, do all to the glory of God" (1 Cor. 10:31).

VIII

PERSONAL PREPARATION

Bullhead Pond was one of my boyhood haunts. It was a beautiful little body of water not much larger than a city block. There must have been literally thousands of fish in this hole because every one of us caught our share almost daily. We also swam in Bullhead Pond, and there was a forsaken rowboat which provided good fun.

The Cedar River flowed within two hundred yards of our favorite fishin' spot and that was the problem. The Cedar was a lovely stream running placidly through the Iowa hills. But then one year, during the spring rains, the river went wild. Its waters left their constraining banks and flooded the country for miles around. Livestock was drowned; homes were filled with mud; and the picture was one of tragic destruction.

At last, after what seemed like ages to us boys, the Cedar returned to her natural level. But Bullhead Pond was never the same again. Our fish were gone. They had escaped to the river. The swimmin' hole was filled with silt, branches, boards, and debris. This was a personal boyhood tragedy for everyone in our gang.

I have thought often about Bullhead Pond as I pondered the words of II Corinthians 5:14 (K.J.V.), "For the love of Christ constraineth us . . ." Most of us are like the Cedar River. We are only as safe as our restraints are adequate. Unless there is some solid limiting factor around us, we become destructive, our peace is destroyed by raging pressures beyond our control, and we bring hurt rather than blessing.

The Christian gospel is "good news" partially because it brings us the glad tidings that this essential inner control is not a do-it-yourself job. Whenever we let him, our Risen Lord comes into our hearts. He masters our inner raging, sets for us safe boundaries, and handles the flow of our lives in their intended channels. By his constraints we become forces for peace rather than destruction. With his control we are what we were created to be.

Colossians 1:27 tells us that Christ in us is the hope of glory. It is speaking, of course, of God's glory, not ours! Therefore we can well conclude that life's number one assignment is to develop rightly in our relationship with the inner Christ. When we make this our aim and forsake all else that our hearts might be his, we have discovered our divine origin and purpose.

It becomes apparent that the church officer's top priority is to yield himself continually to the inner working of the Lord. This is the stuff of prime importance not only for God's Kingdom in our hearts but that we might be "ambassadors for Christ" in every one of our contacts for the church.

The reader has already sensed that this kind of ministry is much too much for any weak human to accomplish alone. But that is exactly the point—we are not on our own. Christ is there in our hearts when we let him be, reaching out to his own through us.

We have emphasized the importance of prayer as a major part of this work. We have also seen that prayer is not some magic formula by which we get what we want from the divine storehouse. Prayer, when it is right, is God getting "the self" out of our central spot that his Spirit might take over and use this life his way.

The quick prayer "Lord, speak through me!" is best prayed out of a deep background of more serious prayer. Therefore it behooves us as leaders of his church to develop a strong inner relationship before we relate our lives to others. We can only represent him right in public if we have been inwardly taught of his presence in the prayer chamber.

The most effective workers in the pastoral ministry of church officers are men of the "Quiet Time." They know how to visit with others because they have spent much time in secret visiting with their Lord.

The Quiet Time may be a morning tryst observed before the

family is up and before human traffic makes its way down the thoroughfares of the mind. It might consist of Bible reading and the study of some devotional classic. Some of it may be spent in self-examination before the white light of Christ's inner searching. It will be given sometimes to talking with him and sometimes to listening as he speaks. Some may find this most effective in the evening when the shadows shut out the day's light and there is a feeling of relaxation. One man, an executive with a major oil company, has his Quiet Time each day immediately following his lunch period. He shuts his door, closes off the phone, and goes to his knees beside his swivel chair. There will always be hope in the land so long as men like this are relating their lives to God in the market place. The main item for an effective Quiet Time is not "when" or "what method" but "whether" it becomes a steady reality in a daily inner relationship.

Obviously, the church officer who is making a vital contribution as a tool of "the Christ within" will be found faithfully at worship. It is not that God is any more present when the corporate body of Christ gathers to sing and listen and pray. Just as a car operates only if it stops for refueling, so regular worship provides the energy for steady service. The leader who worships sets a worthy example and his weekly presence there will witness for good in other lives. But more than this, he is using this means to be inwardly refreshed for more use to his Lord.

The pastoral ministry of the church officer is not a gimmick to win more members to the roll. It is not for "doing better than the Methodists." It is not for keeping people happy nor for assuring the church a stronger income. The real purpose of this service is to win the world to the Lord. It is for creating a Christ-centered Household of God. It is to nourish the flock in an understanding of the Christian life. It is for shaping the church into an instrument of God's holy will. This is our calling; this is our challenge direct from the Lord who did not die for men in the bulk but for each individual soul who is precious to the heart of our Heavenly Father.

Any officer who senses the full responsibility of his election will be thrilled and humbled that he has been called to the Kingdom for such a day as this.

This is his reason for being an officer and this is his prayer for himself and his church:

> ... the Lord make you increase and abound in love to one another and toward all men (1 Thess. 3:12).

IX

VISITORS
AT WORK

"Define the universe and give three examples" was a favorite quiz question of our college philosophy professor. The good doctor would let us struggle with this for a time. Then he would lead into a discussion which invariably brought us to the points he wished to make.

His words still echo down the corridors of at least one student's mind—"There are three 'tools of life's trade' which I would like to sell you in this course. One is a dedicated sense of awe which makes life's mystery bearable. . . . Two is an inner tolerance toward other people who may be just as right as you are even though they are different. . . . Three is the quiet of soul which comes with your acceptance that there is a Power greater than your own which works through you when you let it."

These are excellent "tools of life's trade" for church callers. We have tried continually to emphasize the truth that, as officer-visitors, we are representatives of a Power greater than our own. When we think of all those things which *could* happen in this work, we recognize immediately that our knowledge, by itself, is highly inadequate.

As we go into other homes than our own we do well to carry with us the "inner tolerance" which readily accepts differences in the other person. This flexibility of soul is a great asset for church callers. It puts us at ease and makes the other fellow more comfortable in our presence.

The "dedicated sense of awe," which our professor wished to sell his class, will also be high on the agenda of any officer who hopes to be effective. Some things are highly unexplainable on this side of eternity. Whenever we enter the inner chambers of other minds we do well to realize that we can never know all the answers. True love does not insist on total comprehension. The only phrase repeated twice in Paul's great hymn of love (I Cor. 13, K.J.V.) is the four-word statement "we know in part"! Blessed is the church caller who understands this truth and allows for it in his contacts.

Absolute perfectionists do not make the best visitors. Rigid patterns of mind which insist on their way do well to work through their own problems before inflicting their unyielding selves on others. Such people are likely to create a negative impression for the church. Folks are much more inclined to "cooperate" with leaders who understand our basic Protestant tenet "The Priesthood of Believers." When we grasp this truth we find it carries with it "awe" and "tolerance" and recognition of a Power greater than our own.

The church officer who comes to this final chapter may be tempted to say, "This is too big an assignment for a little man like me." When he reaches this point he is ready to start down the road toward becoming an effective instrument for God's use in his church. All that has been said is to be interpreted in this light. Because there *is* a Power greater than our own we do not wait for perfection before we begin. The "Principles" of Chapter II and the suggestions which follow are not "requirements" for beginners. They are, rather, goals toward which we aim that we might more effectively serve him who fills in by his grace what we lack on our own.

The following sample calls will also be approached in this spirit. They are offered here in the hope that they may be useful for individual analysis or group discussion. They are not presented as shining examples of "how to" but rather as stories of particular calls. The reader will recognize immediately that some of the work is excellent, some is very much the opposite.

The record here is taken from actual calling experiences. Obviously, they do not include everything which was said on that particular visit. Instead, they attempt to present important points for the caller's observation. It will also be clear that each given situation demands a different approach on the part of the caller. In every case there are certain crucial points where the visit might have taken a different turn with a different answer. They reflect clearly the necessity for "awe" and "tolerance" and reliance on a Power greater than the caller's own.

How to Use These Suggestions

Four visits are described at length. Six situations are set down for consideration. Each has been "tested" by a group of church callers who meet monthly at 8:00 A.M. on the second Sunday of each month for reporting and discussion. Although Presbyterians believe that God usually speaks through the majority, every alert believer knows that sometimes this is not so. Yet true to our tradition we move forward together in the faith that God often brings out of our corporate efforts what he wants in the end. These call-situations have been used both by experienced callers and by new recruits. In every case where they were treated at length, the group came out very close to the analysis of "experts" who have examined them and given their conclusions.

For this reason, we do not attempt to deal at length with the "right" and "wrong" of each description. Certain "what to look for" suggestions are offered as helps at the outset. Questions for consideration are given at the end of each of the "visits" described.

Some groups have acted out these visits for the calling committee's observation. When this is done, rehearsal should precede the presentation to make it effective. A simpler method of use is to present one call at a time in printed form, allow time for the group's reading, and then proceed to the discussion. This latter approach saves time and has proven itself equally effective to the role-play method.

Another excellent approach is to ask certain able participants in the program to write up some of their own experiences for the group's consideration. When calls of an especially interesting nature are reported, they might be the subject for helpful material if set down in written form.

In most calls, including those reported here, there may be several different answers containing some truth. This officer went in this direction by his own best judgment. Another might have taken a different route which would have been equally effective. As we have seen, there is no absolute "law of the Medes and the Persians" when making church calls. The best rule is to be ruled by the Spirit of the Lord in all our efforts.

VISIT I

CALLING ON AN INACTIVE MEMBER

Elder Dave Jones has been assigned the Smith family in a general visitation of non-attending members. The Smiths have quit coming to worship. According to the church treasurer they have no pledge to the budget, and there is no record of participation in any of the church's activities. Obviously Dave is on a "first-name" basis with this family through another connection.

(Things to look for: Notice the way in which Dave casually seems to "agree" with objections before he moves into his own thinking. Watch for places where he seems deliberately to keep the conversation from going beyond the Smiths' present ability to grasp the deeper meanings of the church's teachings. See how he aims all he says toward this one end—to get his friends involved in something which might reshape their thinking.)

Dave "Good evening, Harry. I'm calling tonight about the church. May I come in?"

Harry "Sure thing, come in. Have a seat. Haven't heard from the church in a long time. Is it pledge time again?"

Dave "Thanks, Harry; it's good to see you again. No, I'm not here to talk about money. Just wanted to come by and let you know we miss you. I was asking the pastor this week if you've had sickness or been out of town."

Harry "Naw, we really ought to be ashamed, I guess. Just got out of the habit. It's mostly habit you know. Let me call Alice. She's doing the dishes. Alice! Dave Jones from the church is here."

Alice "Good evening, Dave. Nice of you to stop by. I was saying the other day we ought to get back to the church. But we've had so much company this fall. Then Jennie—she's our teenager, you know—had an operation. The little ones had flu, and you know how it goes."

Dave "Sure, I know. It really takes some doing to keep everything going smoothly these days, doesn't it?"

Harry "You can say that again! Seems like we just get one problem solved and up come two more."

Dave "My wife and I feel the same way. But, you know, we find so much help in solving our problems when we attend church every Sunday."

Alice "You do? To tell you the truth, Dave—you don't mind if I'm frank, do you?—we find the church services rather irrelevant. Seems like the preacher talks over our heads and the whole thing misses the point somehow."

Dave "I'll grant you some sermons hit me harder than others, Alice. But let me tell you something we've been doing. We've been having daily devotions. The whole family joins in and we take turns reading our *Day by Day*. We seem to be so much more in tune to spiritual truths when we're faithful to this discipline."

Harry "Boy, I can see us doing that. Whenever do you find time? This is a madhouse in the morning, and I'm never home for lunch. Everybody goes off in a different direction in the evenings. Seems like we don't have time to really live these days."

Alice "You certainly hit the nail on the head that time!"

Dave "I know what you mean, Harry. It's like that sometimes at our house, too. But you know, we've found that daily devotions have a marvelous effect on getting us organized. Seems like they give us a center of reference. It's as if life goes smoother when we let the Lord talk to us and we talk to him."

Alice "But when *do* you find time?"

Dave "Of course every family has to do it their way. But we find it works best at our house while we're still around the table right after supper."

Alice "Guess we could try it, Harry." (No comment from Harry.)

Dave "Tell you what I'll do. I'll bring you by a copy of the devotional guide this quarter. You give it a try for thirty days and let me know what you think. I hope you'll find it a blessing like we have."

Harry "But you know the Bible better than we do, Dave. I'll bet if we knew the Bible like you do we'd be able to understand all this stuff better too."

Alice "Harry's right. Only it sounds sort of weak, doesn't it? I guess you can't know the Bible unless you study it."

Dave "Let me tell you about something else we've done. Mary and I have joined a Bible study group and you're one hundred percent right, Harry. The more you learn the more all this means. Let me call you next time our group meets and we'll come by for you. You'd really love these folks. They're a great bunch."

Harry "But I'd feel so stupid with all those Bible scholars. I'd hate to show my ignorance."

Dave "We're really not scholars, Harry. We're just seekers together, and I'll guarantee you nobody will laugh at you."

Alice "I wish you'd call us like you say. I've felt sometimes that something is missing around here. Maybe we need a new approach. It might be a good thing."

Harry "Be careful, Alice. Let's not get in over our heads."

Alice "But, honey, sometimes I feel like there is something good inside me all shriveled up because I've never fed it. Couldn't we go once or twice? It might be just what we need. I'd sure like to give it a try.

Harry "Guess there's no harm in that. But while we're at it, Dave, I guess we might as well get all our gripes on the table. I got this dun two years ago from the church treasurer and if there's anything that irks me it's the church always asking for money. And then sending those awful statements. That's just too much."

Dave "I'll make you a deal, Harry. You forget about that end of it for a while and come with us to our Bible study group. You'll feel better about giving to the church when you're acquainted with the folks and study with us a while. O.K.?"

Harry "You swing a mean argument, Dave. But I never heard a fairer proposition. We'll go, this once."

Alice "I'm already looking forward to it. Don't forget to call us, will you?"

Dave "I promise! Now I better be going. Have a couple more calls I'd like to make tonight. Thanks for inviting me in. I'll be calling you. O.K.?"

Harry "O.K. Sorry you have to leave, Dave. Sure was good of you to come by. Goodnight."

Dave "Goodnight. God bless you!"

Questions about this call:

1. Note that Dave did not invite the Smiths to church services. Is this a mistake? Why did he take the "study" route and leave worship out of the discussion?

2. What do you think of the technique: "I know what you mean, Harry," "My wife and I feel the same way," "Sure, I know"?

3. Should he have inquired about Jennie and the other children?

Why didn't he ask to see them and discuss their church life with them?

4. Should Dave have defended the preacher's sermons? Is it good to let this slide by as he did?

5. Do you think Dave should have followed up Harry's lead about that "dun" from the church treasurer? Why didn't he?

6. Should he have closed the visit with a prayer?

In your judgment of "effectiveness" should this call be graded:

Excellent_____   Good_____   Fair_____   Poor_____

VISIT II

Bob Little has been assigned to visit John Anderson. John was in an accident six weeks ago. His long hospitalization has left him feeling neglected and very much "out of things." It is obvious that Bob and John are friends through previous connections.

(Things to look for: At what points does it seem to you that Bob isn't even thinking about John and his welfare? Where in this call do you find him expressing a sincere concern for the patient? Look for things which might indicate that Bob is tense and unrelaxed in this visit. Can you find indications that each man changes role as the call progresses? If so, indicate where this took place.)

Bob   (To the nurse at the desk) "Good evening, I'm Bob Little from John Anderson's church. Would it be all right if I visit him?" (The nurse checks his room and ushers Bob in.)

Bob   "Hi, John, how's it going?"

John   "Pretty rough, Bob. Nice surprise to see you."

Bob   "Well, I'll tell you, John—I was assigned your name for a call from the church. They elected me Deacon this year, and everyone has a job to do. Mine's calling. We've missed you, and everyone is wondering when you'll ever get back."

John   "What do you know? I thought the church had forgotten me. Had a lot of visitors the first couple weeks and then they dropped me. Seems like nobody cares much over the long haul."

Bob   "Now you listen to me, John. You're one hundred percent wrong. Why do you think I came if we aren't interested? What's the matter with the pastor? Hasn't he been here?"

John   "Oh, sure, he comes now and then, but he never stays long.

You know how rushed he is these days. But let's don't argue. Have a seat!"

Bob   "I really don't have time, John. How're you feeling anyway?"

John   "Just terrible. My leg hurts all the time and there's this awful pain in my chest. Makes me wonder if I'll ever be all right again."

Bob   "My wife was in that bad accident a year ago, remember? I thought she'd never get well."

John   "Hope she didn't have to stay in the hospital this long. Would I ever give a lot for a home-cooked meal. The food here is just awful."

Bob   Yeah. That's what my wife said. She didn't like the nurses either."

John   "Man, do I know what she means. They wake you up to ask you how you're sleeping. And am I sore from all those shots."

Bob   "Sure thing? By the way, I was talking with Roger the other day. He says things at your office are going right along. Better hurry up and get well. I was sick a couple of weeks last spring, and they almost stole my job from me. I'm just kidding, of course."

John   "Big joke. How's the weather outside?"

Bob   "Pretty muggy. Sure will be glad to see the sun again."

John   "How's Mary feeling now? Better I hope."

Bob   "She's improving all the time but sometimes I wonder if she's ever going to be the same again." (Long silence with no comment from John.) "I wish you could go to the big game with me this Friday. They tell me State has a great team this year. I understand one of our forwards has the mumps and the star center hurt his ankle last week. Sure hope they're O.K. by Friday. I hear the wolves are out to get the coach if they don't win this one. Seems like everything depends on winning these days. Don't know what the world is coming to really."

John   "That's the truth! But let's talk about something else. How are things at the church? Did they get the organ rebuilt? How do you like the new Assistant Pastor?"

Bob   "Well, I'll tell you, John. They didn't get enough money in the organ drive. Seems like lots of the members just gave excuses. I was saying the other day it's no wonder attendance is falling off with that old wheezer groaning in our ears. About the new assistant. He's O.K., I guess. But, like I say, let's wait a while and see!"

John   "How do you like my roses, Bob? The fellows at the club sent them. Flowers sure mean a lot at a time like this."

Bob   "Yeah. But it seems like such a waste. Mind if I smoke, John?

My wife says I ought to quit what with all this cancer scare."

John   "My doctor made me quit till my chest is healed. Sure tough. But I'm determined to do what he says."

Bob   "You've got old Doc White, haven't you? They tell me he's a real bug on this cancer stuff. But you know how I figure it—everybody's got to go sometime."

John   "Helen is bringing the children up tonight. She says they really miss me and I'll tell you one thing I've learned—I'm going to spend more time with the family if I ever get out of here. Seems as if things like this really make you think."

Bob   "Yeah. I said the same thing when I was sick. Only it wasn't long till I was back in the same old rat race."

John   "I guess you're right. Some people never learn. Would you mind mailing a letter for me on the way home, Bob? It's right here in my drawer. It's to Betty. She's away at college, you know."

Bob   "Sure, be glad to, John. By the way, did you hear about the Patterson girl? Ran away from school last week and got married. Is the letter stamped? I better be shoving off. Got to stop by on third and cheer up old Sidney. He had a back operation last week. They say he'll be laid up for months. Some folks never get through with trouble. So long."

John   "So long, Bob. Say something cheerful to Sidney for me!"

Questions about this call:

1. What did Bob do right?
2. Where did he make his first mistake?
3. At any one of these attempts on John's part to improve the climate, what might Bob have said to better the visit?
4. Do you think people like Bob should ever make calls for the church? Why?

In your judgment of "effectiveness" how would you rate this call:

Excellent_____   Good_____   Fair_____   Poor_____

VISIT III

Mrs. Miller is eighty-four. She has been in the membership of the church longer than any living person. Deacon Dick Howard has been given her name for a visit from the officers.

(Things to look for: Note how Dick seems almost immediately to identify himself with an aging person's sentiments. Observe what approaches he takes to make Mrs. Miller feel that her life is still worthwhile. See the tender way in which he brings in those things which interest her most. How much preparation do you think Dick has given to this call?)

Dick	"Good evening, Mrs. Miller. I'm Dick Howard from the church, and I came by to see how you are.
Mrs. M.	"Why, hello, Mr. Howard. Come in and sit here by the fire. What a wonderful surprise to have someone from the church come see an old lady like me."
Dick	"We really do miss you since you've been unable to be with us. Hope it won't be long till you'll be back."
Mrs. M.	"Well, you know there's nothing I'd like better than to walk down that aisle again—or to attend one of the women's meetings—or to hear the children's choir. Yes, I certainly do miss my church."
Dick	"I've heard some wonderful things about your work with the children. You know I'm sort of a new member compared with you. I wonder if folks like you know how much we newer members appreciate the good foundations you laid?"
Mrs. M.	"Do you really mean that, Mr. Howard? That's the nicest thing you could possibly say. Sometimes we feel like the world has gone on and left us. You're very kind."
Dick	"Mrs. Miller, don't ever think you're forgotten. Why, just last week I was talking with our pastor about hiring a new children's choir director. He was telling me about how you led the group for years without pay. He said they never sang better than when you had them."
Mrs. M.	"There you go again. Before you know it, you'll be turning my head. But they were wonderful days for me, too, and I'm only glad I had the chance to be of service."
Dick	"This fire sure feels good. Right chilly outside tonight. Looks to me like you have it mighty comfortable here. Anything we could do to make things a little bit better for you?"
Mrs. M.	"You are the nicest thing. Yes, I'm grateful for a warm home where I can have my things. Seems like the old things get dearer the older you grow."
Dick	"Yes, I know. But I really meant it about whether we might do something for you. Any little things? The officers asked me to find out if we could help you in any way."
Mrs. M.	"I guess I'm the most fortunate person in the whole wide world to have a church which cares so much. But I wouldn't want to be a burden. I wouldn't put anyone out for anything."
Dick	"You wouldn't be putting us out, Mrs. Miller. Sometimes

it does us good to do things for others. Go ahead, tell me what you're thinking. The officers wouldn't like it if I came back with no suggestions."

Mrs. M.   "Well, there is one thing you might do. Only I hesitate to ask. I don't want to burden anyone."

Dick   "I'm sure whatever you're thinking wouldn't be a burden for us. In fact, you'd be doing us a favor."

Mrs. M.   "Well, all right, I'll tell you. Of course, it might be too much to expect. If it's going to be a bother you don't need to do it. But my neighbor, Mrs. Logan, she can't get out either, and do you know what her church did? They brought her a record of one of their services. It was on a record machine of some kind and it was just wonderful. It was like you were right there in church. I got to wondering if someone in our church could get some recordings of the children's choir concert next Sunday. You know I can't possibly get out to hear them. My doctor wouldn't hear to it. But if I could just hear them sing someway that would be the nicest thing ever. I could sit here and think of myself leading them like I used to. I could even invite Mrs. Logan over. Of course, now I know it would probably be a lot of bother and I wouldn't want . . ."

Dick   "Mrs. Miller, you can count on it. I'll personally see that the recording is made and that you get to hear it. Won't be any fuss for anyone and we'll be glad if you enjoy it. The officers want you to let us know any time we can show our appreciation in any way."

Mrs. M.   "Oh, I will. I will. Like I say, how could I ever be so fortunate to have a church that cares so much?"

Dick   "Those pictures over there on the table—they're your family, I suppose?"

Mrs. M.   "Yes, this is my son and his wife and boys. They live in Detroit. He has a big job with a car manufacturing company."

Dick   "Those are sure fine-looking boys. Tell me about them."

Mrs. M.   "They are fine boys, Mr. Howard. The younger one, Douglas, is a football player. He has a scholarship at the University. Gregory, the older one, is a professional flutist. He brought his flute when they came last summer. He played for me. Played real well I thought. Helen, that's my son's wife, has always been so nice to me—just like she was my own daughter. Timothy, my son, is an Elder in his church, and you know how proud that makes me. They're a wonderful church family. Our pastor knows their pastor and he has real respect for him. I'm sure my son is a big help to his church. Wish you could meet them."

Dick   "I wish I could too. They sound like a wonderful family. Maybe we can get acquainted next summer. I know you must be very proud of them. And I'm sure they're proud of you."

Mrs. M.   "Timothy grew up in the church, Mr. Howard. You know what the Bible says, 'Train up a child in the way he should go.' Mr. Miller and I tried to keep him interested in good things, and it always did me good to see the families come in to church together on Sunday morning. Do you have a family, Mr. Howard?"

Dick   "I sure do, Mrs. Miller. Two boys and a girl. Some evening I'll bring Audrey and the children over to see you. It would be an honor to have them know you. I'll tell them all about you when I get home and they'll be eager to come."

Mrs. M.   "Oh, I wish you would. Like I say, you can't possibly know what it means to an old person to have someone stop in now and then. But don't wait too long, will you. When you get my age you're living on borrowed time, you know. Sometimes I wonder why I'm still here."

Dick   "It's because the Lord can still use you, Mrs. Miller. He has some reason behind everything he does. Maybe you haven't finished your ministry to other people. Like me, for instance. It's been a real blessing to me just being in your home tonight. I'm coming back soon for sure and I'll be bringing my family over. Then next week you can count on hearing your choir. I hope you enjoy it. I'll tell the officers how much you meant to me tonight."

Mrs. M.   "Give them all my best regards and tell them how it touched me to know they still remember."

Dick   "Would it be all right if I said a prayer before I go?"

Mrs. M.   "Please do. I would like that very much."

Dick   "Heavenly Father, we are grateful for your wonderful love through all our passing years. Thank you for letting me come here tonight to get acquainted with this saint of the Household of God. May she feel the full blessing of Christ's personal presence every day. We are grateful for her faithful service to our church. We know that one day she will hear from the lips of the Master, 'Well done, thou good and faithful servant.' Bless the lives of these loved ones so dear to her. And above all, may she always feel about her the loving arms of the Good Shepherd. For Christ's sake. Amen."

Mrs. M. "That was just beautiful, Mr. Howard. I know the Lord heard every word and it did my soul good to hear you pray. Don't forget to thank the church."

Dick "Goodnight, Mrs. Miller. I'll be seeing you soon and we'll get the record by next week."

Mrs. M. "Goodnight and thank you again!"

Questions about the call:

1. Note that Dick several times asked what the church could do for Mrs. Miller. Was he wise to press the matter? Should he have dropped the subject when she hesitated?
2. What clues would lead you to think that Dick had found out something about Mrs. Miller before he made this call?
3. Discuss Dick's answer to Mrs. Miller's statement, "When you get my age you're living on borrowed time, you know." Should he have quoted more Scripture?
4. Should he have read the Bible with Mrs. Miller?
5. How would you evaluate his closing prayer?

In your judgment of "effectiveness" does this call rate:

Excellent_____   Good_____   Fair_____   Poor_____

SITUATIONS FOR DISCUSSION

In every call certain statements are made by the family visited which are like signposts pointing to the correct path for the caller. Here are six situations with potential for either success or failure. It is at these "make" or "break" moments that the caller will need to be prayerfully attentive to the direction of the Holy Spirit.

I

You have been assigned to call on a new family who joined the church recently. This may be the church's first official contact in this home. You have been ushered into the den where the family has obviously been relaxing after dinner. Here on the coffee table are some half-finished drinks. The hostess has not had time to remove them after she found that you are from the church. They are both obviously embarrassed and in an effort to size you up the husband remarks, "Guess you caught us this time. But we like to relax with a drink now and then. No harm in a little drink, is there? Guess we're lucky you weren't the preacher. I hear he's pretty old-fashioned about things like this." Both of them laugh nervously, waiting for your answer.

What will you reply?

II

You are calling at the hospital on a man who is reported to be dying of cancer. He is not an old man and after discussing incidentals, he tells you about a visitor he had this afternoon. This caller was from a faith-healing group which regularly sends workers to call on all the patients. He describes the conversation and tells you that his afternoon visitor made this statement: "The Bible says that God will heal you if you just have enough faith." Your cancer-stricken fellow member is obviously upset by this claim of the faith-healer. He asks you, "What do you think about that?"

How will you answer?

III

The Morgan family has drifted away from the church and you have been asked to drop by and express the interest of the officers in their welfare. It is not long until they begin a frontal attack on the problem by telling you they are worried about "all the churches going communistic." They quote from certain popular ultra-conservative papers which have been distributed in the parking lot on PTA night. You saw the papers and read their claims that American churchmen have become "dupes of the Reds." With feeling the Morgans tell you that they have been searching through the church school curriculum. They have found many references which indicate that our denomination is also being "infiltrated." They attack the National Council of Churches and tell you that they cut off their pledge when our General Assembly refused to "come out from among them" and "disavow" the National Council. They make it clear that they have been attending the classes at _____ church where they find considerable companionship in their alarm.

What will you say to the Morgans?

IV

Tonight you are making Evangelism calls. You find yourself in the home of an attractive young couple who have moved into the community recently. They have attended church a few times, and they ask some pointed questions about the service, the pastor, the program for young married couples. Their card shows you that they were members of another denomination in their previous home. After exchanging surface questions, the youthful husband makes this statement: "I get the feeling that you folks are more serious about some things than we're used to. I was just saying to my wife that I'd like to know why your pastor is always talking about missions. Don't all these foreign countries have their own religion? What right do we have to impose our beliefs on them? Don't we all stand for the same thing? Aren't we all heading for the same place?"

How will you reply?

V

The Grahams have been in the church for some time. They have been regular in their attendance although they have not participated actively in its program. You are one of the Elders representing the officers in calls on all members prior to World Wide Communion. When you enter the home you sense that Mrs. Graham has been emotionally upset this evening. Mr. Graham is not here, and his wife invites you into the living room. She offers you coffee, and it is obvious that she hopes you will hear her out. She breaks down soon and begins telling you her problem. She and her husband have quarreled, and he has indicated that there is someone else involved. She tells you in great detail how their marriage has broken down until now he wants his freedom to marry someone else. In tearful description she relates the evening's showdown and explains that her heart is breaking with the threatened divorce. You haven't had much opportunity to say anything in the flood of this tragic recitation. Suddenly she stops you with a series of questions and waits in anxious anticipation for your answer. Her questions are: "Do you think divorce is ever right? What should I do? How can I possibly go on?"

What will you say?

VI

This call has brought you face to face with two teen-agers in a home where you have been assigned to call. The mother broaches a touchy problem when she says, "Bob and Mary have lost interest in the church lately. They used to go regularly to church school and the youth meetings. But now they say none of their crowd goes any more and the meetings are nothing but a bore. We don't know what to do with them." Bob and Mary have been listening to all this and the atmosphere is tense. You are apt in your use of humor so you have said something to "clear the air." Then you discover that they are among the legion who still go to church services but their other interests are definitely on the wane. You draw them into a discussion of their complaints. You do a good job of this, and they voice their resentments freely. Finally, Bob sums up their attitude with this cryptic comment: "The teachers are all squares, dad! And those youth meetings. Ugh! All they do is yak a bunch of junk nobody cares about anyway. Why should I set there and get stiff when there's all this good stuff on TV? Why do we all have to be holy Joes anyway? I think Mom is making a federal case out of nothin', don't you?"

What can you answer this brazen young modern?

Religion that is pure and undefiled before God and the Father is this: to visit orphans and widows in their affliction, and to keep oneself unstained from the world.

James 1:27